PIANO • VOCAL • GUITAR

2015
CHRISTIAN HITS

Produced by
Alfred Music
P.O. Box 10003
Van Nuys, CA 91410-0003
alfred.com

Printed in USA.

ISBN-10: 1-4706-2394-3
ISBN-13: 978-1-4706-2394-4

CONTENTS

BACK TO YOU

Words and Music by
ALAN POWELL, BRAD DAMAS
and EVERETTE SMITH

6

BEAUTIFUL

Words and Music by
BEN GLOVER, DAN BREMNES,
DAVID ARTHUR GARCIA, ED CASH
and SCOTT CASH

Gtr. tuned down 1/2 step:
⑥ = E♭ ③ = G♭
⑤ = A♭ ② = B♭
④ = D♭ ① = E♭

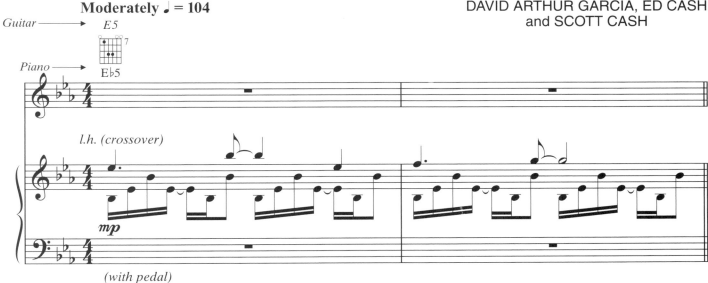

Verse 1:

1. Lord, I want ev-'ry-thing,

ev-'ry-thing You've got for me.

Beautiful - 9 - 1

10

Verse 2:

so beau - ti - ful.

2. Lord, I give You ev - 'ry - thing,___

an - y - thing_____ you want from___ me._____

Take my past and my___ fu - ture, I____ lay it at___ Your___

E5
E♭5

B(4)
B♭(4)

A(9)
A♭(9)

14

GREATER

Words and Music by
BARRY GRAUL, BART MILLARD, BEN GLOVER,
DAVID ARTHUR GARCIA, MIKE SCHEUCHZER,
NATHAN COCHRAN and ROBBY SHAFFER

Moderately, with a half-time feel ♩ = 116

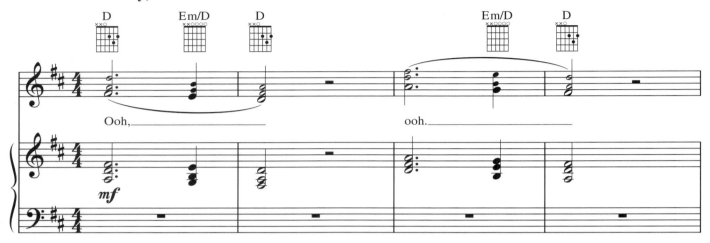

Ooh, ooh.

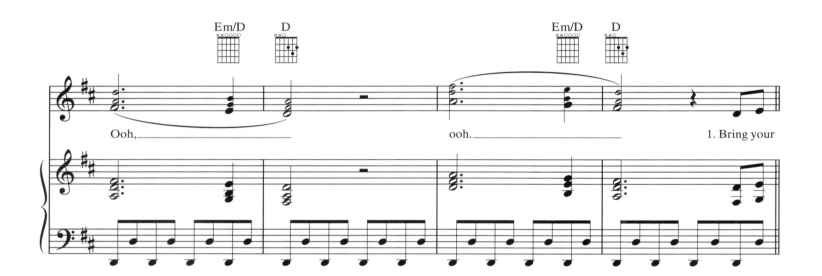

Ooh, ooh. 1. Bring your

Verse:

tired and bring your shame, bring your guilt and bring your
doubts and bring your fears, bring your hurt and bring your

Greater - 7 - 1

22

Bridge:

There'll be days__ I lose the bat - tle, grace says__ that it does - n't mat - ter

'cause the cross__ al - read - y won the war.__ (He's great - er. He's great - ter.)

I am learn - ing to run free - ly, un - der - stand - ing just how He sees me,

and it makes__ me love Him more and more.__ (He's great - er, He's great - er.)

HE KNOWS MY NAME

Words and Music by
FRANCESCA BATTISTELLI,
SETH MOSLEY and MIA FIELDES

*Original recording up 1/2 step in Gb, capo 6th fret.

He Knows My Name - 6 - 1

30

He Knows My Name - 6 - 5

JESUS LOVES ME

Words and Music by
BEN GLOVER, CHRIS TOMLIN
and REUBEN MORGAN

Moderate rock ♩ = 88

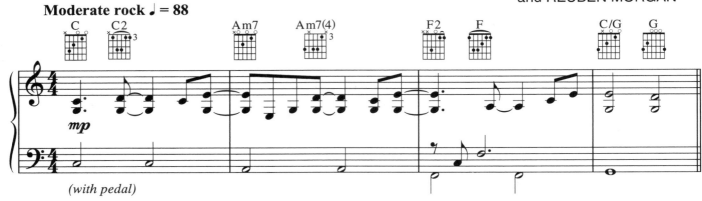

(with pedal)

Verse 1:

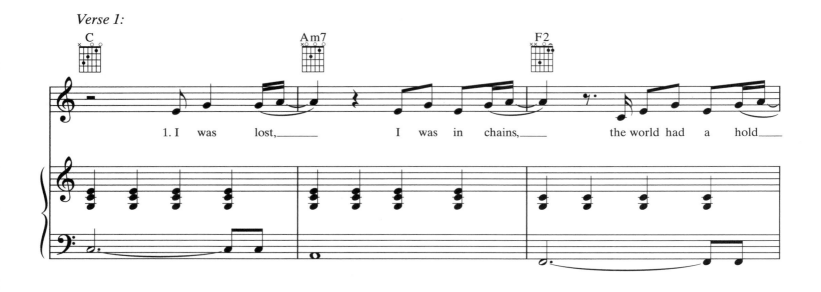

1. I was lost,_____ I was in chains,_____ the world had a hold_____

_____ of me.____ My heart was a stone,_____ I was cov-ered in shame_

Jesus Loves Me - 6 - 1

KING OF MY HEART

Words and Music by
CHRIS RADEMAKER, DAVE BARNES,
JEFF PARDO and JODY KING

Moderate pop rock ♩ = 92   *Verse 1:*

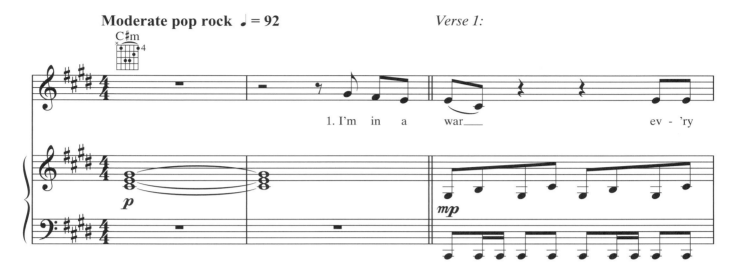

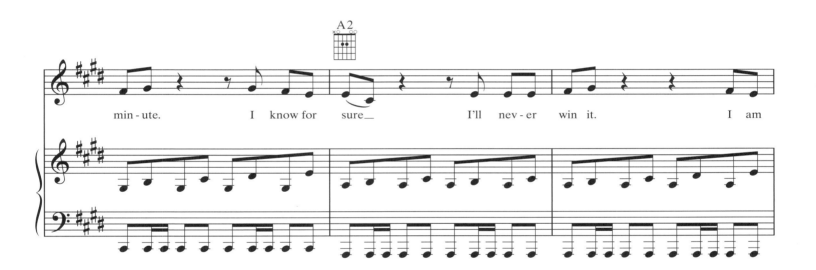

40

44

King of My Heart - 7 - 6

MADE NEW

Words and Music by
JOSIAH JAMES, LINCOLN BREWSTER
and COLBY WEDGEWORTH

Made New - 6 - 1

MORE OF YOU

Words and Music by
BEN GLOVER, COLTON DIXON
and DAVID ARTHUR GARCIA

Verse 1 (Sing 1st time only):
1. I made my cas-tle tall, I built up ev-'ry wall.

Verse 2 (Sing 2nd time only):
2. This life I hold so close. Oh God, I let it go.

This is my king-dom and it needs to fall.

I re-fuse to gain the world_ and lose my soul._

More of You - 6 - 1

More of You - 6 - 2

56

Chorus:

More of You,___ less of me.___ Make me who___ I'm meant to be. You're all I want,

___ all I need,_ You're ev-'ry-thing._____ Take it all, I sur-ren-der;

be my___ King.___ God, I choose_ more of You_ and less of___ me. I need more of

More of You - 6 - 5

MULTIPLIED

Words and Music by
NATHANIEL RINEHART
and WILLIAM RINEHART

Moderate rock, with African tom feel ♩ = 115

Verse 1 (Sing 1st time only):

1. Your love is___

Verse 2 (Sing 2nd time only):

(2.) love is___

like ra-di-ant dia-monds___ burst-ing in-

like ra-di-ant dia-monds___ burst-ing in-

Multiplied - 9 - 1

60

Multiplied - 9 - 2

62

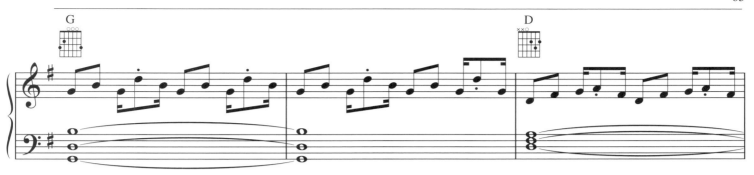

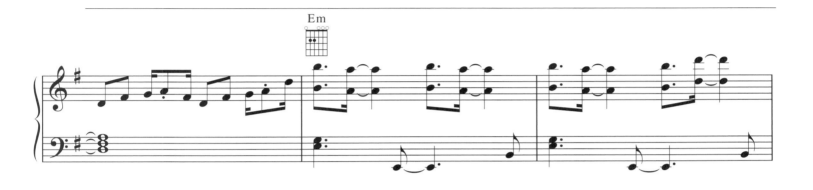

2. Your

Multiplied - 9 - 5

64

plied.

66

Multiplied - 9 - 8

Multiplied - 9 - 9

OVERWHELMED

Words and Music by
MICHAEL WEAVER
and PHIL WICKHAM

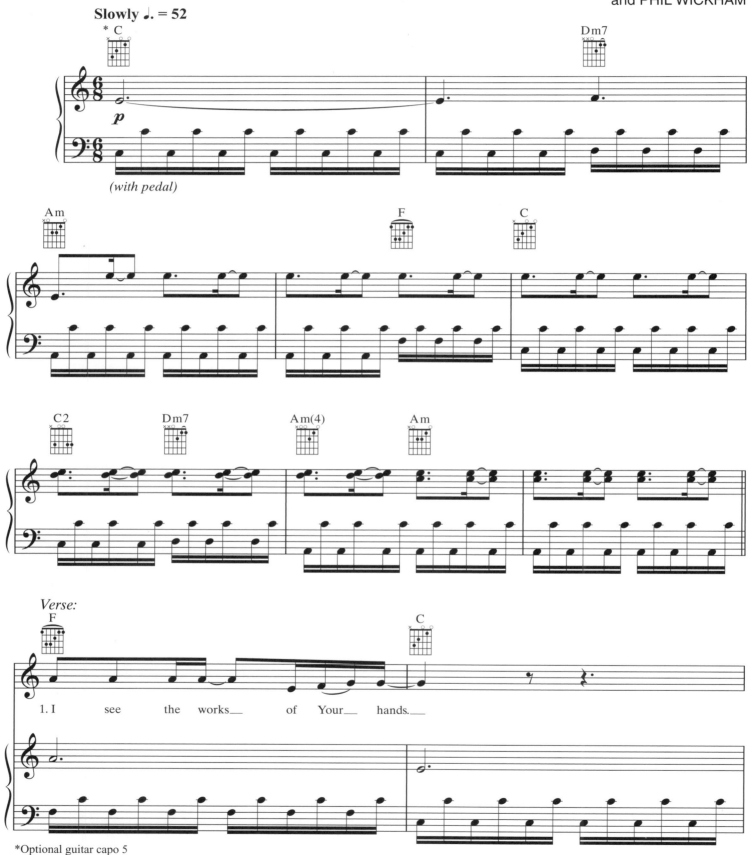

*Optional guitar capo 5

Overwhelmed - 10 - 1

72

SOMETHING IN THE WATER

Words and Music by
CARRIE UNDERWOOD, BRETT JAMES
and CHRIS DeSTEFANO

Something in the Water - 10 - 1

'Just a lit-tle faith,___ it-'ll all___ get bet-ter.' So I fol-

___ love pour-ing down from___ a - bove,___ got___ washed___

lowed that preach-er man down___ to the riv-er." And now I'm

___ in the wa - ter,___ washed___ in the blood.___ And now I'm

Chorus:

changed.___

82

Bridge:

86

START A FIRE

Words and Music by
CHAD MICHAEL MATTSON, SETH DAVID MOSLEY
and JONATHAN BURTON LOWRY

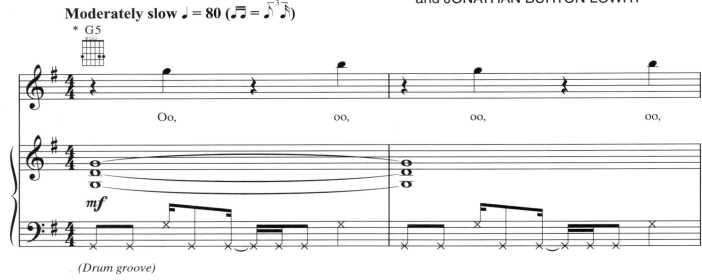

(Drum groove)

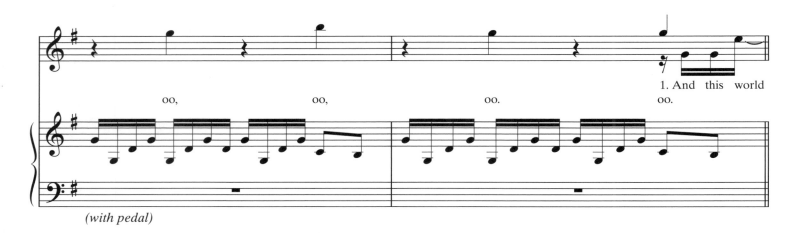

(with pedal)

Verse 1:

_____ can be cold and bit-ter, feels like___ we're in the dead of win-ter,

*Original recording up 1/2 step in A♭.

Verse 2:

WE BELIEVE

Words and Music by
MATTHEW HOOPER, RICHIE FIKE
and TRAVIS RYAN

Moderately slow ♩ = 66

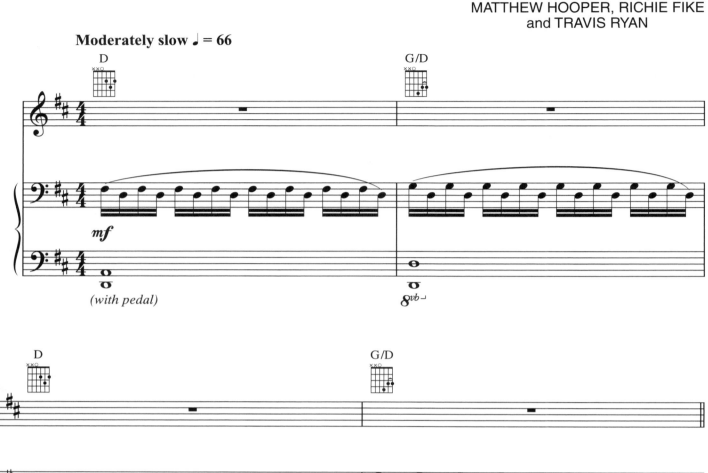

(with pedal)

sim.

Verse 1:

1. In this time_ of des - per - a - tion

We Believe - 9 - 1

Verse 3:

Chorus:

YOU AMAZE US

Words and Music by
JORDAN MOHILOWSKI, MATTHEW ADCOX
and DOUGLAS FOWLER

Moderately slow ♩ = 82

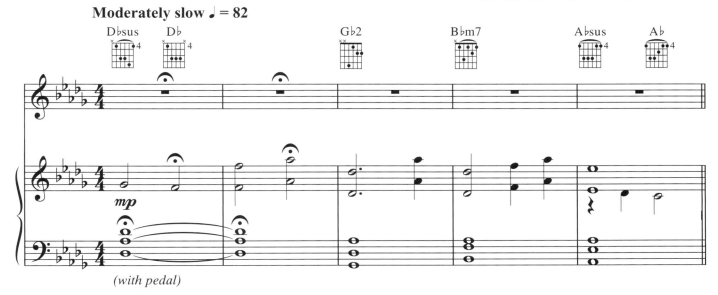

(with pedal)

Verse 1:

1. You are___ our life___ when death is all___ a - round. You are___ our___ peace___

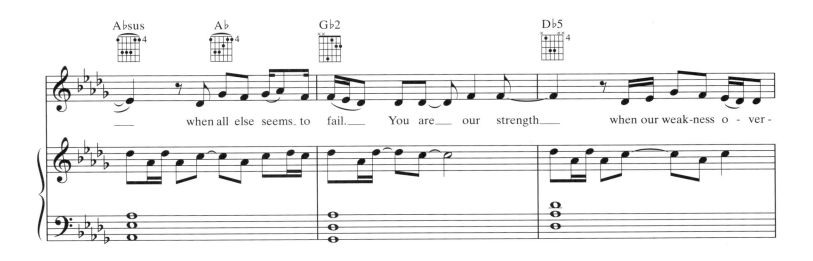

___ when all else seems___ to fail.___ You are___ our strength___ when our weak-ness o - ver-

YOU MAKE ME BRAVE

Words and Music by
AMANDA COOK

Verse 2:

114

118

You are not a-gainst us. Cham-pi-on of heav-en, You made a way. Cham-pi-on of heav-en, You made a way for all to en-ter in.

You Make Me Brave - 9 - 9